Creating Transcripts for Your Unique Child

Help Your Homeschool Graduate Stand Out from the Crowd

Lee Binz,
The HomeScholar

First Printing, 2018

Printed in the United States of America

Cover Design by Robin Montoya
Edited by Kimberly Charron

ISBN: 9781791947477

Disclaimer: Parents assume full responsibility for the education of their children in accordance with state law. College requirements vary, so make sure to check with the colleges about specific requirements for homeschoolers. We offer no guarantees, written or implied, that the use of our products and services will result in college admissions or scholarship awards.

Creating Transcripts for Your Unique Child

Help Your Homeschool Graduate Stand Out from the Crowd

What are Coffee Break Books?

Creating Transcripts for Your Unique Child is part of The HomeScholar's Coffee Break Book series.

Designed especially for parents who don't want to spend hours and hours reading a 400-page book on homeschooling high school, each book combines Lee's practical and friendly approach with detailed, but easy-to-digest information, perfect to read over a cup of coffee at your favorite coffee shop!

Never overwhelming, always accessible and manageable, each book in the series will give parents the tools they need to tackle the tasks of homeschooling high school, one warm sip at a time.

Everything about these Coffee Break Books is designed to connote simplicity, ease and comfort—from the size (fits in a purse), to the font and paragraph length (easy on the eyes), to the price (the same as a Starbucks Venti Triple Caramel Macchiato). Unlike a fancy coffee drink, however, these books are guilt-free pleasures you will want to enjoy again and again!

Table of Contents

Introduction

Unique Situations

A transcript is a one-page overview of your child's academic record. Any student who plans to go to college needs a transcript and even students who don't plan to attend will benefit from this record of their high school courses. A homeschool transcript can demonstrate your student's strengths, depth, and individuality. It can combine all the wonderful educational experiences of high school into one centralized location on paper.

You are Not Alone

Families have a lot in common, but every family is unique. Some might say homeschool families are especially unique! When I speak about uniqueness in families, there are often tears in the audience because parents are afraid their special family situation has never been experienced by anyone else; they don't know how to create a transcript for their student in this unique situation and think they may fail at homeschooling.

I'm a homeschool mom like you and I have homeschool friends and homeschool clients. Every one of these people is unique. I have spoken with thousands of homeschoolers and have heard it all—almost every possible situation! Believe me, at this point I am not shocked by anything! It's not my place to judge anyone's unique family situation. I am never appalled or disappointed and I don't gossip, laugh, or lecture.

My goal is to support and encourage all homeschool parents, no matter the situation. I'm here to share my experience and expertise with you so you can successfully navigate your personal situation.

In all my experiences with homeschool families, I've found that no situation is so unique that it makes them all alone in the whole wide world. Instead, I see the same *unique* situations repeatedly and I see people who feel as if they're alone. You're not alone and I can help. Let's get started!

Chapter 1

Course Grading

The first key concept you need to know is how to give a quick grading estimate. An *A* or 4.0 earned in a course can mean that your child works to mastery in your homeschool and has met your high expectations, your child has high standardized test scores (e.g. an 80 or 90 percent on the Iowa Basic standardized test), or your child loves the subject (a good reason to give an *A*).

A grade of *B* or 3.0 means your child did well but their work wasn't worth an *A*. A grade of *C* or 2.0 is when your child does not do well. I often say that a grade of *C* is when their work is *stinky* but they kept progressing to the next level. You know your student has passed when they keep going on to the next level in a course.

When we homeschooled, only half our classes involved tests for evaluation and the rest involved quick estimates, yet colleges loved our transcripts and records. You can go through all sorts of contortions if you want to, but it's not important, especially not when colleges only perform a quick review of your child's transcript. My son once told me that my grades were bogus because I used my quick grading estimate. However, in college he found out I was a tough grader compared to his college professors!

Bad Grades

Sometimes children earn bad grades or completely bomb a class in school. If they're in a public or private school, they usually don't have another chance to learn the material to improve their grade and it goes on their transcript. Your child's homeschool transcript only needs to include your student's successes, not their failures.

I often don't tell people that one of my children flunked "Algebra 1" the first time he studied it in high school. When he took "Algebra 1" again, he earned an *A*. His transcript shows he received an *A* in "Algebra 1" but not that he failed the first time. I only gave him a grade for the final homeschool class, which he excelled in.

If your student completely bombs a class in a public or private school, you could get them to repeat the class, or take it again at home. You could also provide test scores instead. For instance, if your child fails a biology class, give them an SAT Subject Test in biology and provide the test score instead of the failed class score.

It can be helpful to include an explanation of such situations in a cover letter. The cover letter is usually included with the transcript. If your child has bad grades, a cover letter is your opportunity to explain the situation. You may need to explain that your child was bullied in school, suffered consequences, and you removed them from the violent situation and began homeschooling. Or you may need to explain major medical or emotional problems. You can mention that when they started homeschooling, your student developed a love of learning.

Flunking School

Of course, sometimes there are bad **years** instead of merely bad grades and your child is flunking school completely. I see this when a client is withdrawing their child from public school. A cover letter can be helpful to explain exactly what happened: why you decided to withdraw them, the benefits you experienced, and the problems at school.

Sometimes a student performs poorly because they don't care and weren't challenged enough. Your child can repeat classes or you can replace these classes. Even better, as a homeschooler you can modify your curriculum or use a different curriculum that fits your child's learning style.

Sometimes, when a child comes out of a difficult public or private school environment, they need some time to decompress. If this is what your child is going through, I recommend reading the book, *Deschooling Gently*. Not all children need this time—sometimes children haven't been academically challenged and do better when you challenge them right away. But for other children who experienced difficulty, a time to decompress can be a good idea.

If a student is flunking out of public or private school, it is not necessary to include those classes on their homeschool transcript. You can instead let the school transcript speak for itself. Normally, I suggest placing all school classes on the homeschool transcript because it is the clearinghouse for all a child's educational activities. However, if you experience an entire flunked school year or two, sometimes it's better not to include these grades on the homeschool transcript to bring into sharp contrast the differences between the two school environments. In general, if they make your child seem smarter, include non-homeschool classes on your homeschool transcript but if they do not make your child look smarter, let the public or private school transcript speak for itself.

If your child has flunked out of school, you do need to send the public or private school transcript to each college upon application, which is why the cover letter can be so helpful. But this doesn't mean you must automatically put it on the homeschool transcript. If your child repeated the class, course descriptions are strongly encouraged because colleges will want to know what you used for the class and whether you did a thorough job teaching your child.

You might also want to consider additional testing. If your child flunked, show that they have a high school amount of material before moving on. Colleges may ask for work in the student's handwriting. If they flunk math and you re-taught math, the math section of the SAT or ACT can demonstrate competence, but a college may still ask for a math paper in the student's own handwriting.

Straight *A* Students

At the other end of the spectrum are the straight *A* students. Many parents feel uncomfortable giving their own children straight *A's* but I've seen colleges ask parents to raise their child's transcript grades so they match the test scores. If your child is earning high test scores, make sure you give them good grades.

It's okay for a homeschooler to earn straight A's. Many homeschoolers work to mastery, and mastery often means straight A's, so many parents award straight A's on their children's transcripts. Give your child marks that reflect their work.

Colleges like to see straight A kids, because a college's business is evaluated based on the grade point average of students they get to attend their college. If the grades arc honest and true, colleges prefer that you have a straight A student rather than giving them a bunch of B's to make them look normal. I encourage you to be honest and true and award straight A's if your child is a straight A student.

Chapter 2

Course Credits

If your child is working one hour or more per day, one whole textbook in a year, or too many hours to count, it's one credit. Too many hours to count happened when my children were on the swim team and reached about 300 hours in one year and I thought it would be crazy to count hours. One full credit is represented as 1.0.

A half credit means your child has worked half an hour per day, two to three hours per week, or a total of 60 to 75 hours. Half credits are represented as 0.5 each.

Not Enough Credits

What happens if your child does not

earn enough credits? First, beware of misconceptions. Are you sure they don't have enough credits? Six credits per year is certainly enough, as students attend five to seven classes throughout the year at many schools.

Remember that formal curriculum isn't required to award a credit. You can include natural learning in any credits included on the transcript. If your child is learning music through piano lessons or engaging in P.E. through skiing, put these activities on the transcript. When parents say their children don't have enough credits, I ask whether they included delight directed learning and any P.E. activities.

If you feel your student barely has enough credits, ask yourself "have they earned enough credits to meet college admission requirements?" If they have met the college requirements, then they have enough credits.

Of course, there are times when students don't have enough credits. In this case, you can add an additional year of school and organize your child's transcript by subject rather than by year. Instead of stating your child took Algebra 1 in freshman year and Algebra 2 in sophomore year, simply list their four math classes. This way, you're not highlighting the fact your student took an additional year of school.

When your child hasn't earned enough credits, don't be too focused on weaknesses but do fill any gaps you notice. Take an additional year and try to fill up those credits. Make sure to focus on their weaknesses or any credits they didn't want to complete.

Too Many Credits

Some students have *too many* credits. A normal college prep transcript includes 20 to 24 credits but it's not unheard of to earn 35 to 45. It's unusual, but not unbelievable.

If your student has too many credits, certainly more than 45, it might be a little excessive. First, you can reduce electives that aren't truly academic in nature. If your child has 46 credits, "Home Economics" or "Driver's Ed" can be left off the transcript. You can also remove some half credit classes, especially if they aren't significant academically or significant to your child's uniqueness.

Sometimes you can combine experiences, such as including a one credit class of hula dancing as part of another dance class. Even if the student is taking multiple dance classes, roll hula in with the other dance classes and consider it all one credit of dance, noting in the course description that the dance course includes hula.

Some colleges place a limit on how many college credits they want to see from a student enrolling in first year. If the student has racked up several college credits, they may not be allowed to enroll as a college freshman. They are usually only referring to college credits taken at a community college or an online college or university. This doesn't mean that your child's 26 high school credits will jeopardize their freshman status.

It is important to pay close attention to college rules. If a college policy jeopardizes freshman status, it could mean your child cannot earn freshman scholarships. Of course, it also could mean your child graduates early, so they may not need freshman scholarships. It could also mean missing out on freshman housing. Colleges usually reserve spots for freshmen in dorms so they don't need to find an apartment on their own when they're only 18 years old. This is important to consider, especially if you're from out of town.

If your child has earned too many credits, sometimes a college will want them to declare a major as a college junior the day they arrive at school. This could be a big decision for an 18-year-old to make on the first day of school if they haven't been set on a major already.

Chapter 3

Delight Directed Learning

Delight directed learning usually translates into an elective or a specific subject your child loves. For example, if your child loves taking piano lessons, this might be counted as a music class. My son loved chess. We counted this as an elective (critical thinking) since it wasn't a core curriculum course.

In the midst of your child's delight directed learning, make sure the core subjects are covered. Cover math and science even though your child likes other subjects more. It is okay for your child to earn multiple credits each year in the same subject. This demonstrates the expertise and uniqueness in your child, which is desirable to colleges. You want your child to look unique and different.

One parent had a child who planned to take five years of a 4-H Veterinary Science class starting in middle school. A professional in the field told her that all the materials in this five-year vet science program were at the college level. At the end of the five years, a student would earn 2,000 hours in the veterinary clinic with 500 hours in the clinical lab. At the end of this five-year experience, the student would be eligible to earn a vet assistance certification.

The parent's question was how to include this delight directed learning on a transcript. "Veterinary Science" is a great starting point. Simply Google the phrase and try to find a college offering a similar program. Veterinary Science is a perfectly acceptable title for a high school class or you can use the same title as the course. In this instance, I would call the course "Veterinary Science with Lab."

You could also place this course under the Early High School Credits portion of your child's transcript. Because it's college level and the student started it in middle school, it could be included as an early high school credit. If your student plans to earn vet assistance certification at the end, instead of calling it "Veterinary Science with Lab" you might call it "Honors Veterinary Science" or "Honors Veterinary Assistant Certification."

This course should be listed on the transcript as a class each year because the child took it each year but should also be included on the transcript activity list. On the activity list (usually at the bottom of the transcript), you might include it as, "Amarillo Veterinary Clinic Volunteer 9, 10, 11, 12–Certified Veterinary Assistant 12." In this way, you take delight directed learning and put it on the transcript as a class as well as an activity.

In a course description, you might indicate the scope of this incredibly huge experience. For instance, "For this course, one high school credit is determined as 300 hours of study and 100 hours of clinical lab time."

Incorporate Delight Directed Learning

If your child is not involved in veterinary science and you're wondering how this applies to you, then here is a little formula for incorporating delight directed learning into your own homeschool. Write each of your student's unique, delight directed learning activities on a separate sticky note. Group these sticky notes together by similarities until you have groups big enough to count as a high school credit. Remember, there's no double dipping, so you can't use the same sticky note for two different classes. But it is okay for you to use one experience as a class *and* as an activity.

I was involved in choir every year at the public high school. My transcript included "Choir" every single year and I earned one credit of choir. When they asked me to put my activities on my transcript, I included choir. It's okay to include a course on an activity list and as a credit.

Special Needs Students

Usually when parents ask about their special needs students, it's because the child is behind in most subjects or the student has dyslexia (reading challenges), dyscalculia (math challenges), or dysgraphia (writing challenges). If this sounds like your child, you will find help at Learning Disabilities America (LDAmerica.org).

When considering learning challenges,

make sure you consider the whole person. Don't hold a child back in all subjects for the sake of one subject. If your special needs student is in high school, everything they do in high school should be put on the high school transcript. Even if your child is behind or has a learning disability, you still put their high school classes on the high school transcript.

Sometimes a student's standardized test scores are below average. It typically won't make sense for this student to have earned straight *A's* in highly academic classes, but it might make sense to have earned an *A* in a remedial math class.

A degree in a major such as business is not highly technical, so many students with special needs are able to go to college for business. I would never discourage anyone from doing so. If your child is significantly below average, it might take extra time for the community college to get them up to speed but they can still do so. Often, parents feel as if their child is significantly below grade level, but in reality they are not.

Two of my best friends' three boys have quite severe learning disabilities. Her 18-year-old struggled with spelling three-letter words. He performed poorly on standardized test scores and was far below on the SAT and ACT, so she chose not to provide those scores to colleges. Instead, he entered the workforce at Starbucks.

He realized that although he had a learning disability, he was still smart and decided to go back to community college and take the classes he needed. Then he transferred to a university, got excellent scholarships, earned a degree in business, and is now working in an excellent job doing what he wants to do. A disability doesn't mean you have to hold your child back from their goals.

Gifted and Advanced

On the opposite end of the spectrum are gifted and talented students. These students also need to cover the core courses but try to do so with topics they like. If you can capture their delight and incorporate it into core courses, they will have more time to pursue other interests. A cover letter can help explain delight directed courses your child engaged in naturally.

It's important to make sure that test scores match classes, especially if your child is young. If you try to demonstrate that a class in 5th grade is worthy to be on the high school transcript, providing test scores such as a high SAT score in math, can corroborate the high school designation.

Tests can be used as documentation to prove that a child is advanced or gifted. Consider having your child take an SAT Subject Test, AP, or CLEP. You have unlimited class options with a gifted and talented child. If they were in school, your child would be limited by what the teachers wanted to teach, but in you homeschool you are not limited by a teacher's interest. You can provide a wide variety of classes for your child's interests, from the study of mushrooms or birds, to digital photography or forensics. I've seen kids involved in all these interests.

If you have transcript confusion, simply be honest and true, no matter how funny it looks. If you're not sure whether it's true, think about what a private or public school would do. If your child were in public or private school, how would the course be included on the school transcript? Apply it to your unique situation.

Chapter 4

See the Whole Child

Parents are acutely aware of their children's failures. You often see your child as they used to be. They might be almost ready to graduate but you still see them as a youngster; you remember when they fell off a bike or couldn't read. You think back and, in your head, still label your child as a slow reader or not coordinated.

Sometimes it's hard to see where they are at their current age. You become blinded by memories of their childhood. I encourage you to take a step back and make sure you're remembering your child's strengths and not only looking at their weaknesses.

Normal Children

For parents with relatively *normal* children, what does it mean to incorporate the whole child into the transcript? Never compare your child to others. When you see other students' transcripts, all you usually see is the good stuff. This is because when you put together a transcript, you only include the *good news*—your student's success and not their failures. To be honest, most kids look good in black and white. When you only put the good stuff on a transcript and don't include their rotten attitudes or failing subjects, almost every student looks good. The key is *not* to focus on other people's children.

Recently, I heard from a parent who poured out her heart. She asked if it was possible for a child to simply do high school level courses in high school and college level courses in college. Her daughter wanted to forget about going to college because she "wasn't smart enough." This mom was worried because she felt that all the transcript examples were for gifted children. Although some are, most transcripts are for completely normal children who look fabulous because their accomplishments are laid out in black and white.

This mom shared some of her child's positive attributes but completely and unknowingly discounted them. She reported her child's annual test scores in the 80 to 90 percent range but worried they wouldn't do well on the SAT or ACT. However, a standardized test score is a standardized test score—if your child scores high on one, they will probably score high on another, so this student would probably do well on the SAT.

She said her child was a better writer as a 9th or 10th grader than she or her husband, even though they both had advanced degrees. That is some seriously good writing. She also reported that her child had played in a high school symphony since 8th grade, accumulating 200 hours per year!

This mom worried because her child didn't learn Latin in the 5th grade and was concerned that French was slow-going. Hardly anybody learns Latin in the 5th grade and French can be flat out slow-going for everybody. Although this child attended a music camp and a government camp, she "hadn't done any work in a fishing camp." You can't compare what your child has done to what others have done. Otherwise, you might as well compare yourself to the entire Olympics team!

Missing College Prep Classes

If your child has missed some math or English classes, it's important to teach them. Whatever the subject, teach them at their level. Don't hold your child back in school because they're missing one kind of class. Frequently, I hear parents say their children aren't at high school level because they haven't started "Algebra 1" yet. Some students will be behind in math; don't hold them back in high school simply because of their level of math.

Encouraging Your Student

It can also help to separate each academic area in your head. If your child has a hard time in math, don't teach sciences that include math concepts. If your child has a difficult time with writing, don't include writing in their other classes and don't consider it a way to evaluate them.

Teach your child in their love language—the way they learn best. You might teach without writing, if necessary. You might move forward in other subjects even if your student can't get beyond Algebra 1. They can still learn economics, biology, P.E., or English without knowing Algebra 1.

You can also teach typing, especially for the child who has difficulty writing. Or consider purchasing a dictation program such as Dragon Naturally Speaking, which allows your student to speak each lesson as it is typed for them. Assign writing practice only when covering English skills but not necessarily in biology or history. If your student is a poor reader, consider teaching them using mostly videos or books on tape so they don't need to read everything.

Chapter 5

What Would a Traditional School Do?

When you face academic questions in your homeschool, it's sometimes helpful to ask yourself what a traditional school would do. This is a great way to avoid confusion and think simply about the problems you face. Think about what would have happened when you were back in high school.

Activity or High School Course?

Let's apply this to your child's unique transcript. I often get questions such as, "Is this an activity or a high school class?" It could be both. As I mentioned, my choir class was both an activity and a high school course for me.

Not all activities are classes on the transcript, though. Your student may be involved in babysitting or training service dogs, but those are not classes you can include on the transcript. Activities they engage in can be included only on the activity list and still have value.

Multiple Credits in One Subject

Your student might accrue multiple high school credits in one subject area. In public school, multiple credits in a single subject can be common because students can register for any class if they have the pre-requisites. I have seen homeschool students do much of their music in a public school. One child took choir, orchestra, and band, so she earned three music credits every single year. It was on her high school transcript from the public high school. If it's okay for the public school, it's okay for homeschoolers, too!

An English example from a public school might be a child taking journalism, working for the yearbook, and working for the student paper. A student might take journalism plus English. If you use two complete English programs to teach your child (which I don't recommend for most children), then your student can earn two English credits for the year, as they would in public school.

Chapter 6

Classes Outside the Home

Often, students take a few classes outside the home or at community college during senior year. If your student takes classes outside of your homeschool, it can be helpful to use an acronym to indicate them on the transcript. Choose a two or three-letter acronym and place it in front of the class title. Be sure to define it at the bottom of the transcript.

Whether your child completes an honors geometry class online or a watercolor class at a co-op, at the bottom of your child's transcript, define the terms. FVA might refer to Florida Virtual Academy for an "FVA Geometry" course. HHC could refer to Highline Homeschool Co-op for an "HHC Watercolor Painting" class. Some parents even include a three-letter acronym for classes taught at home, but I don't recommend this.

Co-op Classes

Let's apply the concept of using an acronym for co-op classes, since many kids take classes at homeschool co-ops. If your child does, remember that they are not official school grades. If the class is not at a school and does not provide a transcript, then those grades are only *serving suggestions*, even if they are taught by certified teachers.

Parents determine each transcript grade for co-op classes. Your student may attend a co-op one day a week, but parents evaluate four days a week. You may choose to indicate their co-op classes on the transcript by including an acronym (e.g. HSC Homeschool Co-op) in front of the course title. Some parents make a mention of the co-op in their course descriptions instead of on the transcript.

Part-Time Classes at School

You might also use a three-letter acronym on a transcript when your student takes part-time classes at school. If your child takes a class at a brick-and-mortar school (whether it's accredited or not), the school will provide a transcript. When they do, use the school's transcript information and add it to your child's homeschool transcript. This includes the same class title, class number (if included), and exact final grade.

Of course, not all schools use the same grading scale; one might use A, B, C, while another uses 1, 2, 3. If this happens, it's okay to adjust it to your grading scale. Make sure to adjust it accurately. In addition, reflect the same class credit, remembering that a whole year is one credit and half a year is a half credit.

Dual Enrollment or College Classes

Dual enrollment is probably the most common way I see students taking classes outside the home. These classes should go on your child's homeschool transcript using an acronym, including the exact title and class number. For example, my children took art at Highline Community College, so their transcripts included, "HCC Art 100: Introduction to Art" and "HCC Math 124: Introductory Calculus." Use the same grades the college assigns. Again, you can adjust them to your own grading scale. This doesn't mean you have to go down to two decimals but do reflect the numbers or letters the school assigns.

Previous Schools

Sometimes a parent withdraws their

child from public high school and wonders how to reflect this on the homeschool transcript. First, remember that the school transcript must be sent from the high school directly to colleges during the admission process. But you can also list those classes on your child's homeschool transcript. You should include a previous school on the transcript when it makes your student look smart. Include good grades because they will enhance your child's transcript.

However, if your student has failing grades, you might want to mention in your cover letter that the freshman year grades will arrive from a public high school and keep them off the homeschool transcript. Then colleges can see that even though freshman year is blank, they can expect to see grades on a separate transcript. Remember, you are the academic clearinghouse for your children; everything educational they do can be included on the high school transcript (but doesn't have to be).

Chapter 7

No Double Dipping

Although an activity can be included on both the transcript and activity list, one hour of study can only be counted for one class. You can't use the same hour for credit in two different courses. If your child spends 150 hours in one subject, that makes one credit; another 150 hours might be counted toward another credit.

Some classes take many hours, perhaps even more than 150. Math is a good example. When your child gets to the high school level, math takes a long time. Students come home from public school and often do two hours of math homework. This can happen in your homeschool, too. You teach them math, they work for an hour in the morning, and then they may have homework at night.

Some classes are simply *big* classes. Call it one hour and don't overthink it. If you use only one textbook for the class, then definitely make it only one credit, even if it takes more than 150 hours.

Some classes, though, are *small*. When I was in high school, we reviewed the concept of supply and demand in an economics class. Most of the class was spent filling out the 1040 EZ and that was almost all we did the whole semester. The class required little. Some classes require a lot and some classes require little, but each hour of your homeschool can only be used once for each class. Again, it's okay to include it on the transcript *and* the activity list, but use it for credit in only one class.

Similar Classes at Different Times

Sometimes kids take similar classes at

different times, which does not count as double dipping. One parent I know had a child who took "Algebra 2" at home and then went to community college and studied algebra. You need to ask yourself what happens to public school students in the same classes. If a course were taught in high school, it would go on the transcript and if it were taught in college, it would go on the transcript. High school algebra and college algebra are not the same.

Another example might be biology and advanced biology classes; they're not the same. Some public schools teach biology one year and then an AP biology class to the same students the next year. These students end up with two biology classes on their high school transcript. For similar classes at different times, it's not double dipping and they can all be included on the transcript.

Classes Covering Many Subjects

Double dipping also comes into play when classes cover many subjects. I call these *behemoth* classes and they usually happen when the curriculum covers multiple subject areas. I used the Sonlight curriculum, which included English, history, and Bible studies every year. The easiest way to determine how much credits these behemoth courses count toward is to look at the information provided for credit value. Usually, a class claims to cover a certain amount of history, philosophy, and literature. Use the information given to divide it out.

This is not double dipping—the curriculum creators have set out exactly how many high school credits the curriculum provides. Sometimes the curriculum includes literature, composition, vocabulary, spelling, and grammar, in which case you will see that these are all parts of English and you can include them all in one English credit as you divide the behemoth class into its subject areas and groups.

One thing to keep in mind is to avoid overwork and burnout for your child or yourself. A curriculum may include huge amounts of work. As the parent, you will know when it's a crazy amount and can cut out portions you know are more than enough for a high school credit. Lastly, if you use a behemoth curriculum, take something out of equal value anytime you supplement or add to the curriculum. For instance, if you use Sonlight and add an Institute for Excellence in Writing course, you should subtract the Sonlight curriculum writing portion. Otherwise, you will cause burnout by requiring your child to do too much.

Classical Education

Another instance when double dipping might happen is when using the classical method of education, which uses a four-year rotation for history and geography. Colleges want to see some standard courses on a student's transcript, so it's important to give courses standard names. There are many styles of classical education and four-year curriculum, but if you look up the topics you're studying, often you can come up with a course title and a credit value that reflects what you do and provides a standard course name.

An example would be calling a course, "Ancient World History and Classical Literature" or "Medieval World History and British Literature." If you're studying the revolutionary period, you might call it "American History" or "Foundations of American Government." You could call a modern history class, "Economics and Government."

I encourage families who use a classical method of education to make sure they cover biology and chemistry. Sometimes they'll study other branches of science instead, such as astronomy or physics. But a child who is thriving in a classical education environment is usually college bound. If they're thriving, this typically means they like learning, enjoy a challenge, and want to go to college. Studying biology and chemistry will open their prospects a little more. Biology and chemistry are especially important to take in high school if your child wants to go into science, technology, computers, engineering, math, medicine, or a similar field.

Chapter 8

Cover Letters Cover Problems

Cover letters can be used to explain a lot of the craziness of your homeschool. Colleges usually read these before the transcript, so you can warm them up to any issues your student might be facing. If there are any major issues, you can explain what is unusual and try to highlight the positives.

Often, when people experience craziness in their lives, they feel as if it's a huge detriment and don't see how it can be positive. Whatever your craziness is, try to think about it in a positive light. For example, when a homeschool family moves mid-year, they might focus on how unique their child's education was, instead of how they couldn't homeschool during that crazy time. Look at your situation in the best possible light and present it this way in the cover letter.

Five-Year High School

Sometimes parents ask me how to convey their five-year high school plan. It's not unusual for students to take five years of high school—it happens in public schools, too. And it's not that unusual for a high school student to graduate as late as the age of 20. One way to handle this is to wait until your child is ready to graduate high school and then count backwards; the last four years become their high school years. It's like students who start kindergarten a year or two late because they were young, immature, or premature.

Sometimes you need all five of those years to show that your student completed enough courses. If this is the case, explain your purpose for completing high school in five years in a cover letter. Simply explain that your child is ready for college. Demonstrate college readiness by showing your child took an online class or spent an extra year to level up writing skills and colleges will accept this.

If your student took five years to graduate from high school, explain that you wanted to make sure your child didn't need any remedial classes in college and they are now ready across the board. Colleges are used to admitting students who don't have everything they need to go to college, though. Statistically, between 30 and 40 percent of smart students who are admitted to college are at a remedial level in something. They may need remedial classes in English or math. Most schools give a test during the first days of college to see if a student needs remedial help and then place them in a remedial class if needed.

Major Medical Problems

If you're facing major medical problems, either in your family or your extended family, remember that you are not alone. Major medical problems can happen even when you homeschool high school. Focus on the health issues first. If your child has a severe medical issue, it's important for them to recover. Graduating from high school is less important. Focus on the *now*, which allows you to give these issues the priority needed.

Before the illness, perhaps you thought your child would attend an honors college program or Ivy League school. Now, major medical issues have come up and it's time to understand that average is okay in high school. Remember that easy is okay, too; some classes are hard and some classes are easy. If you need to teach economics the easy way or teach American history using videos, it's completely acceptable.

I know quite a few children with serious head injuries or major medical problems that meant being bedridden for a year or two. If this is your family situation, remember what your child did before and go back to what a school would do. If your child has a head injury now but two years ago they had a great year of high school, you still put that year on the transcript.

If your child was in public school and got in a car crash, that year on their public school transcript would not go away, it would still be there. After the event or the illness, you'd be teaching your child at their new level, but you would still put their past courses on the transcript. If your child completed Algebra 1 or Algebra 2 before their illness but afterward are only able to accomplish business math, it's perfectly fine.

If your child is facing major medical issues, think about what you can do with them now instead of what you can't do. Give your child some cozy couch time, snuggled up while reading aloud or watching educational videos. Even though they're lying on the couch, they're learning through educational activities. They're still able to get some of their school work done. Whatever they accomplish can be counted on their high school transcript.

Major Emotional Issues

The same holds true when it comes to major emotional issues. If you or your child are facing major emotional issues, you need to think *safety first*. Don't try to do school. If your child needs psychological help, be sure they get the counseling they need. You don't want your child to become suicidal in your effort to graduate them on time. Live your life without regrets and get your child help when they need it.

You can scoop up any credits they

accumulate naturally and focus on other credits later. School is not as nearly as important as the life, health, and well-being of your child. Get family and individual counseling because when your children grow up, they may not agree to go.

When experiencing major emotional issues, sometimes deschooling is important after you bring your child home from public school. This means letting them have a break from schoolwork, or perhaps only doing school work that won't stress your child out. If they have obsessive-compulsive disorder or major anxiety, then it's not the time to teach calculus.

If these emotional issues have come up and an entire year of school has passed, don't assume all the learning is gone. Your student might have tried and failed often, but some of that learning may still be there. Consider assessing your child. If it's appropriate, given the emotional issues at hand, assess your student using subject tests to see if they have learned enough from classes. Provide subject tests and give a pass-fail grade.

There are two ways to assign credits: count credits by the number of hours a student worked or based on what they learned by the end. Instead of focusing on the 180 hours that weren't done, see if they can pass a test and then give credit and a grade based on it.

Chapter 9

The Love Languages of Colleges

As you create your child's transcript, make sure you speak colleges' love languages of grades, credits, and GPA. At the same time, recognize that you do not have to change your homeschool at all. School at home is not required to collect grades, credits, and GPA, but you must explain things thoroughly and translate your homeschool into the love languages of colleges.

Unschoolers Outside the Box

I often get questions from unschoolers who homeschool outside the box and want to put the best spin on their homeschool but don't want to use tests.

Tests are not necessary to learn. You can evaluate students without using tests. But I do encourage you to give your child either the SAT or ACT, because no matter how your child translates onto a transcript, colleges will also want an SAT or ACT score.

When you consider how to evaluate, think about everything your student does that you call "school." We only graded tests in math, foreign language, and science. Those curriculum came with tests, so it was mainly a matter of convenience for me! For all 28 of our other classes, I used different ways to evaluate my children.

What did they do for daily work? In English, I evaluated their reading and writing. For reading, I decided to grade in areas such as reading, discussion, analysis, and research. And for writing, I evaluated every paper and listed each one by title or topic (Emancipation Proclamation, for example). I didn't *grade* each paper, I simply edited it when they were done and sent it back to them for corrections. Once it was done to my satisfaction, I gave them 100 percent.

Sometimes I didn't list the titles of the papers they wrote. Instead, I listed the *kind* of papers they had written: essay, research report, short story, or poetry. Finally, I decided that the testing they did each year for their annual assessment also counted as an evaluation. The areas covered on those tests were vocabulary, comprehension, spelling, mechanics, and expression. For each of these items, they scored at grade level or above, which met my expectations and earned another 100 percent.

At times, it's appropriate to show the nuances of your grades to colleges because you want to demonstrate that your homeschool's 4.0 is not a number you pulled out of thin air. Demonstrate thoughtful consideration of your evaluations and show your standards and methods of grading. Then let each college decide how they will use the grades, knowing you did your best to provide them with the information needed.

What Do Colleges Want to See?

Colleges usually want to see standard courses on a transcript.

English

Most colleges like to see four years of English, which you can cover in a variety of ways. Your student can study literature and composition through a curriculum. Or you can simply assign reading and writing to do daily. Consider a speech class as an alternative. Keep in mind that what really matters is ending up with a student who enjoys reading, communicates effectively in writing, and knows how to learn.

Math

Math is such a cornerstone for other subjects, careers, and college majors, that I believe it's important to include four years of math. Most colleges require at least three years, and many want four years. They like to see students moving forward in their math studies, so teach your student consistently at their level.

Science

Three years of science is expected for college preparation, with at least one that includes a lab. Each area of science is so different that a child may detest one but love another, so it's helpful to expose them to different branches of science. You can also try unique subjects such as geology, astronomy, or computer programming. Colleges love to see these more unique courses, so don't be afraid to delve into another area of science if your child shows an interest.

Social Studies

Colleges like to see three or four years of social studies. They often further specify which classes they want to see. Usually this includes world history, American history, American government, and economics. Remember that you aren't confined to teach only the expected classes for social studies, either. One of our sons took a course in Russian history and the other chose psychology.

Foreign Language

Many colleges require a foreign language for admission. Usually the requirement is two to three years of a single language so the student is reasonably fluent. Ensure your student works on the curriculum a little each day. A daily 15-minute study period is more effective than one hour once a week. Use a foreign language curriculum designed for homeschoolers so you aren't expected to already know the language. Let the student learn independently and check on their progress periodically.

Physical Education

Some children find it easy to earn the required two credits of P.E., while others balk at physical exercise. Unique ways to obtain physical education credits include yoga or weight lifting classes taken at the YMCA. Your kids could also take CPR classes or study health. Some kids who hate P.E. love swing dancing or video games requiring movement. Any physical activity that breaks a sweat counts!

Fine Arts

Colleges like to see fine arts on the transcript as well, but usually one credit will suffice. Fine arts include music, art, theater, and dance. My students studied fine arts through history using library books. We studied music history by checking out CDs and biographical books on different composers and styles of music.

Let Them Learn

Alternatively, you can allow your child to learn subjects intentionally at community college when they become an adult. Whatever you decide, remember to *translate*, not change the classes your children learn naturally. Simply be honest and true about what they accomplish.

Conclusion

Prepare Them to Leave Home

You're not only preparing a transcript, you are preparing your child to leave home. Homeschooling will end and your child will grow up, leave home, and live on their own. They need adult survival skills. Whether they're skills that can be added to their transcript or not, these survival skills are important.

Saying Goodbye

When you take your child to college, it's one step on the path to independence. Other steps follow, such as: the first summer away from home, the first post-college apartment, and the first holiday away from home. Saying goodbye at college is as important as other goodbyes. Each step brings its own emotions, ranging from tears to relief.

I noticed one thing as I said my goodbyes at college—I had no regrets. I knew without a doubt that my children were academically prepared as well as prepared for any assault on their worldview, and that I had shaped and molded their characters and behaviors to the best of my ability. Their lives were up to them now.

All parents experience deep emotions when sending kids to college—not only homeschoolers do. When you feel a tug on your heart, it's not because you are a homeschool parent but simply a parent. Your heart may hurt, but homeschooling is a healing balm. Homeschooling high school can minimize your regrets once your children are raised. With the ability to shape and mold character while educating them, your children have the best possible chance of success. Letting go can come with no regrets!

Handle the Hand-off

When setting your children off into the world, here are three pieces of advice.

1. Keep your five-year plan in mind.

In five years, you want to have a happy, healthy, close, extended family. When conflict occurs during college, keep the five-year plan in mind.

2. Step in only when your child is being life-threateningly stupid.

They will make poor choices, but they can learn from them, as you and I do every day. Believe me, being life-threateningly (or life-alteringly) stupid happens—not often, but it happens.

3. Remember your scripture.

One of the most popular Bible verses relevant to homeschooling will still be your greatest encouragement after they go away to college. Proverbs 22:6 says,

"Train up a child in the way he should go, and when he is old he will not depart from it."

Homeschool parents are responsible for the first portion of the verse. The Bible instructs us to "train up" our child. The Lord promises us a reward for our work, "he will not depart from it." When you send your children into the world, you are in the middle of this verse, at the comma—a dramatic pause. There is a pause between training your child up and the promise at the end which is your child's responsibility. That's the part where you are letting go. Let go of your responsibility and look with great anticipation to the "when he is old."

On a personal level, I hate that pause. I wish the promise was immediate and that children who have been brought up in the "fear and admonition of the Lord" would never stray from the path. But you and I know this isn't true. Grown children make bad choices—sometimes a confounding string of bad choices. At that point, you need to remember one important fact—they are now adults and adults get to make their own choices, as we did.

The Four Seasons of Homeschooling

Homeschool parents assume four primary roles throughout their childrens' lives: caretaker, teacher, mentor, and friend. The last season of homeschooling—which promises to last the longest—is the season of friendship. Finally, you and your child are equals. You may find yourself learning as much or more from them as they do from you.

When the kids are grown and gone, take a deep breath and relax. You have a wonderful, lifelong friendship to look forward to. The key to enjoying this friendship is you—you need to stop homeschooling your child. Provide guidance and counsel when asked but hold back on unsolicited advice. Enjoy their friendship. You deserve it. Job well done!

Appendix 1

Question and Answer

Question: *We have lived in a different country for most of the last nine years. There are a lot of traveling experiences, both throughout the country and in about five other countries, so my children have that type of experience as well as a foreign language. How do you include these cultural experiences?*

Answer: It's like delight directed learning except it's forced on them a bit, as it wasn't their choice to go to China. Consider what you did in your host country and what you learned while you were there. It doesn't matter whether they're in China or Taiwan or Uganda, they're still doing the same thing—learning. Military families often dive into the culture and study everything. They try to learn the language as best they can, study the history, and tour about the country.

If this expresses your experience, you can put one credit on the transcript each year such as "Language and Culture of Japan." Or perhaps you moved halfway through the year and it would be the "Language and Culture of Japan" for half a credit, and the language and culture of Brazil for another half a credit. Google "course description Japan" and see what pops up—you might get some unique ideas. Many colleges send kids for study abroad and give the children college credit for what they've learned simply living in the country. They include all those experiences into a college credit, so high schools can do so, too.

Question: *Concerning double-dipping for high school credits, if we're taking both world history and English, is it* *okay for the student to write some history essays as English writing assignments, and have those count for time spent on English and history course work?*

Answer: Remember that some classes are difficult, and some classes are easier. If you use one of those behemoth courses which jumble together literature and history, I understand, because we used Sonlight. I took the papers they wrote and divided them in half. Half of the papers were put into the history pile and the other half went into the English pile and I would not double dip. Homeschoolers often think there needs to be tons of writing in every class but that's not necessary.

Question: *Why do we have to include work samples with our transcripts? How do I do this and what should I include?*

Answer: You never know what colleges are going to ask for. When you keep records for homeschool, I encourage you to keep pieces of information for every class. If a college requests an English paper in the student's handwriting, provide it. If you provide work samples with your transcript, only include a small handful, one to three work samples. Make sure they're the best of your student's work—the ones you thought were worthy of an *A* or perhaps won awards. It's like applying for a job; you wouldn't put down somebody who hated you as a reference.

Question: *Is it honest to tweak transcripts for different colleges? Do people ever highlight different classes for the different colleges they apply to?*

Answer: I encourage homeschoolers to make transcripts as appealing as possible to their first choice college. At the same time, don't forget which transcript you submitted to each college.

Don't tweak it so you end up with 12 different transcripts to give to 12 colleges. Instead, tweak your child's transcript so it's the most appealing to your number one college and keep it the same way to apply to all the other colleges as well.

I also encourage parents to create a transcript by subject *and* by year because some colleges will want it by year and some will want the information by subject. If you format it the same way for all colleges, it cuts back on the guess work and you don't have to think about what class title you called a class for a specific college.

Your child's homeschool transcript is an *official* transcript, so keep it in one format and not a variety of formats. Don't tweak it for every college; tweak it as necessary using those college facts you know but only create one transcript that you provide to all colleges.

I almost sent the wrong son's transcript when I submitted them to colleges. It is easy to mix up transcripts, so don't have more than one transcript to keep track of.

Question: *For senior year grades on both the course description and transcript, do I put, "To Be Determined" or do I put the estimated finish date?*

Answer: You do want to include the classes they take for senior year on the transcript even when you submit it in September and they haven't even started the classes yet. In a public school, the moment the class is registered, it goes on the transcript. There's no grade but they will indicate the class title, subject area, and credit value. You can either put "IP" for in progress in place of the grade or "TBD" for to be determined but everything else will remain the same.

Colleges understand that in a public school, sometimes a child intends to take a class but when the class is full, they can't. In a community college, sometimes a student will intend to take a calculus class but couldn't get into the class, so they end up taking a business math class instead. They understand that this happens.

If you intend to teach your child a subject and they ultimately can't or don't take it, colleges will understand. It's not written in stone until the grade comes in. Colleges also want to know what the student is planning to take and make sure the child is still challenging themselves in their senior year.

Question: *Will you touch on the one-page versus two-page transcript? I can't get rid of the legitimate classes my child took to make room, but I don't have room for test scores and there are few activities on the one page.*

Answer: One-page transcripts are always preferable; two pages are only rarely suggested. Sometimes a two-page transcript is suggested when a child has way too many credits, including community college classes, and they are all racking up.

Sometimes, when a child has an ordinary amount of work and what really energizes them is extracurricular activities, then those activities will go on endlessly, making a two-page transcript necessary. Even if the child has 22 credits, they may have accomplished many activities, which compensates for it.

If you think your child's transcript could possibly fit onto one page, you can shrink down the font to 12 or under. On my transcript templates, some of the font is 16 or 14 for headings, so you can change everything down to a 12 to make more room. Sometimes you can even put class names down to a font size of 10. Never go below a font size of 10, though, as it becomes illegible for admission clerks to read, which makes them less likely to want to award admission and scholarships. You may be able to find a template that doesn't have as much white space, which can shrink it to one page.

To get down to a one-page transcript, you might want to group classes together. You could group half-credit classes into one-credit classes, so they take up less room. Remove the unimportant. Test scores aren't always important; not all schools put test scores on transcripts.

If you give too much information about each activity, that can make the transcript much too long. The transcript is merely for the smallest possible mention of each one, only four or five words at most about each activity. It's helpful to include a second page that lists your activities with all the details: how many hours, where each was located, and whether your child had a leadership position.

Question: *What is the best way to document P.E. when combining black belt classes with regular family exercises such as P90X? Do we use pass-fail or give a grade using some kind of evaluation?*

Answer: You could call it P.E. to combine both. Or consider the sport he's a black belt in and the P90X as his practice training for that activity. If he's doing Tae Kwon Do, the P90X is what keeps him fit so he can earn his black belt in Tae Kwon Do; your class would then be called "P.E. Tae Kwon Do."

I always encourage parents to include a grade for all homeschool classes. Colleges have told me they prefer grades. Some colleges don't like homeschool grades and may decide not to use your homeschool grades but it's still up to you to put down a grade.

The brutal truth is that colleges look at

the test scores, make a decision about your child's academic prowess, and then look at the transcript. If they're admitting your child, they want to see those grades, so they can award scholarships and admission.

When you put a pass-fail grade on the transcript, some colleges interpret that pass-fail grade as a *C* which is a far cry from an *A* and can do some damage to your child's GPA. If they decide to recalculate the GPA and make all your pass-fail grades *Cs*, that will be a problem.

I encourage parents to include course descriptions for every class. If colleges want to know how you came up with an *A* for P.E., it's a good idea to include a course description to explain it's a combination of Tae Kwon Do class where he earned a black belt plus he engaged in other activities like P90X as a supplement. List all these activities and give him a grade for them.

If your child meets your expectations, then give them an *A*. If they don't meet your expectations but their efforts were better than most, give them a *B*. And if they really stunk up the field and did a terrible job but kept moving forward, then give them a *C*.

Question: *How do you know if your child is flunking homeschool? My daughter is struggling in several areas. I'm having trouble getting her caught up. Do I have to repeat everything for next year or is time for me to throw in the towel?*

Answer: Homeschool parents can be the hardest graders on the planet. Sometimes homeschool parents think if their child is not getting an *A*, then they're flunking. If your child is getting below a 70 percent on all tests across the board, then it might be worth repeating the subject. But if your child is never going to get better and if there's a serious issue, then call 70 percent a *C* and put it on the transcript.

Usually, you don't see kids flunking because flunking means they're not learning anything. Flunking means they're performing below 70 percent, they're not doing the work, and they're not picking up the book. It implies a relationship parent-teen problem more than a problem with education. This often boils down to the parent having expectations of perfection. It's important to remember that anytime you include a grade, you shouldn't base it solely on the test because no other school grades solely on the test.

Appendix 2

How to Write Perfect Course Descriptions

Some colleges say they don't need course descriptions. but most colleges require, request, or appreciate course descriptions. A wise homeschool parent will maximize scholarships by writing perfect course descriptions for core classes, electives, and delight directed learning.

Why Colleges Want Course Descriptions

A student's high school record is the most important factor in college admission decisions. Grades and the academic rigor of classes are even more important than SAT or ACT scores.

Studies show that the academic rigor of the high school curriculum is the single best predictor of success in college (www2.ed.gov/rschstat/research/pubs/toolboxrevisit/index.html).

Your homeschool course descriptions provide proof that your curriculum is challenging. Course descriptions include details that show that your child succeeded with this challenging curriculum and earned a solid GPA using rigorous material. This is why you create course descriptions.

You do not have to use a school-at-home curriculum or provide classroom instruction with outside teachers. Instead, you can continue to provide a normal, natural home education using the curriculum and learning style that fits your child and your family. At the same time, parents can learn to take this awesome real-life education and transform it into words and numbers in course descriptions colleges understand.

In my experience, homeschool course descriptions can make the difference in earning scholarships. Colleges would rather not give scholarships, of course—they don't want to create any impediments to paying full price for college. For this reason, sometimes colleges say, "No, thank you." Sometimes you need to work extra hard to get scholarships. The more information you can provide about your homeschool, the more they understand the value of home education.

If you are ready to get started, I have created a comprehensive tool to help you complete homeschool records quickly and easily, so you can help your child win scholarships. Check out the Comprehensive Record Solution at comprehensiverecordsolution.com.

Ingredients of Perfect Course Descriptions

When it comes to course descriptions, the more information you can provide about each class the better—as long as you don't go over one page. I suggest each description include three main ingredients.

1.   A paragraph describing what you did

This portion describes the academic rigor of the class, including the topics covered and your study methods.

2.   A list of what you used

The list could include textbooks, natural learning, or a mishmash of curriculum. It should include resources you used intentionally, but also those you used accidentally by following rabbit trails or going on field trips.

3. A description of how you evaluated your child

This is the part of the description that shows how the child performed. It should include natural evaluation and not only tests.

Within these main ingredients, there are many ways to provide information about your class. Some parents go into detail for each one and others don't. However, it's normal to include one paragraph per section and one page per class. More than one page per class is too much. If your course description doesn't include a class title and a list of what you used, then it's too little.

Three Writing Prompts for Course Description Paragraphs

The first portion of a course description is a descriptive essay. In other words, it's simply a 5th grade writing assignment. It's true! You taught your 5th graders to write a descriptive paragraph, and you can do it, too. Write this course description paragraph the same way you taught your child to write a descriptive paragraph. Start by using a writing prompt so you have a framework, and then you can be more creative later, as you become more comfortable.

These three writing prompts will help you describe what you covered in each high school course description.

1. "In this class, the student will . . ."

This prompt gives you the verb tense and point of view of the writing style, so you don't get stuck figuring out if it should be past, present, future or past perfect tense.

2. "The student will study _____ with _____."

This prompt helps you focus on what you are writing and why. Fill in the blanks. For example, "The student will study Algebra with Saxon Algebra 1 by

John H. Saxon Jr."

3. "Topics include _____"

This prompt helps you use the table of contents to construct a major portion of your course description. List topics from the textbook table of contents or online curriculum descriptions.

As you are learning to write a course description, I suggest you begin with the easiest course description, such as math, for which you use a textbook. Then you can combine all the descriptions together. For example, your description might look like this:

In this class, the student will study the concepts of Algebra 1, using Saxon *Algebra 1* by John H. Saxon Jr. Topics include . . . (grab all those freakish math words from the table of contents and insert them here).

Four Ways to Describe Homeschool Evaluation

Teachers in schools have 30 or more students to evaluate and need tests to assess learning. Homeschoolers are not hemmed in the same way. Our evaluations can be done primarily through natural assessments. We can watch what our children do, evaluate what they know, and grade what they produce.

Homeschool grades should always include a variety of ways of evaluating, but each homeschool parent will have a unique way of describing how they determined a grade for each class, using their normal, natural homeschool process for evaluation.

As you describe your grades, you can give an overview of what you are basing your grade upon, like this simple overview.

1. Overview

Grading criteria: 40% Tests, 40% Daily Work, 10% Midterm, 10% Final Exam

Or you can simply provide a conclusion with the grade that was ultimately earned, like this example.

2. Conclusion

Final Grade for Algebra: 94% = A

You might decide to give a blend of overview information and final grade. You can describe what was evaluated plus the final grade.

3. Blend

Tests and Exams 60%, Classwork and Homework 40%. Final Grade for Algebra 1: 94% overall for 4.0

Or you (like me) can provide detailed grading criteria with individual grades and scores for each test, quiz, or paper. This description would list all test scores and all report grades, providing the most detail possible.

4. Detailed Grading Criteria

Here is an example.

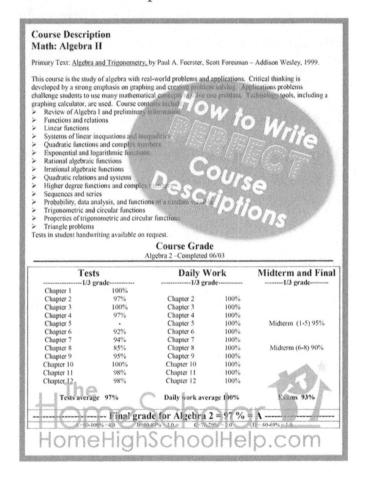

Course Description
Math: Algebra II

Primary Text: Algebra and Trigonometry, by Paul A. Foerster, Scott Foresman – Addison Wesley, 1999.

This course is the study of algebra with real-world problems and applications. Critical thinking is developed by a strong emphasis on graphing and creative problem solving. Applications problems challenge students to use many mathematical concepts to solve one problem. Technology tools, including a graphing calculator, are used. Course contents include:

- Review of Algebra I and preliminary information
- Functions and relations
- Linear functions
- Systems of linear inequations and inequalities
- Quadratic functions and complex numbers
- Exponential and logarithmic functions
- Rational algebraic functions
- Irrational algebraic functions
- Quadratic relations and systems
- Higher degree functions and complex numbers
- Sequences and series
- Probability, data analysis, and functions of a random variable
- Trigonometric and circular functions
- Properties of trigonometric and circular functions
- Triangle problems

Tests in student handwriting available on request.

Course Grade
Algebra 2 – Completed 06/03

Tests		Daily Work		Midterm and Final
----------------1/3 grade----------		-------------1/3 grade----------		--------1/3 grade-------
Chapter 1	100%			
Chapter 2	97%	Chapter 2	100%	
Chapter 3	100%	Chapter 3	100%	
Chapter 4	97%	Chapter 4	100%	
Chapter 5	*	Chapter 5	100%	Midterm (1-5) 95%
Chapter 6	92%	Chapter 6	100%	
Chapter 7	94%	Chapter 7	100%	
Chapter 8	85%	Chapter 8	100%	Midterm (6-8) 90%
Chapter 9	95%	Chapter 9	100%	
Chapter 10	100%	Chapter 10	100%	
Chapter 11	98%	Chapter 11	100%	
Chapter 12	98%	Chapter 12	100%	
Tests average 97%		**Daily work average 100%**		**Exams 93%**

----------- Final grade for Algebra 2 = 97 % = A -----------
A = 90-100% = 4.0   B = 80-89% = 3.0   C = 70-79% = 2.0   D = 60-69% = 1.0

HomeHighSchoolHelp.com

When I wrote course descriptions, I tried to provide every possible individual grade I could within a grading table. I wasn't perfect, though. I lost some tests, quizzes, and lab reports and then I either left them blank or didn't mention they were missing—as if I'd intentionally not used that test.

Provide course descriptions any way you can—short or long, whatever works. I think any way is fine and the more information you can provide, the better.

Getting course descriptions done can seem overwhelming but it doesn't have to be! Follow my six steps and you'll be on your way to completing them in no time.

1. Cut and paste.

Cut and paste is much easier than compose and create, so use descriptions from others when you can. This is why I provide hundreds of course descriptions

in my Comprehensive Record Solution (www.comprehensivesolutions.com).

Within the Course Description Collection, you can use "Control-F" to find the specific description you need.

2. Copy from products purchased

You can copy descriptions from course curriculum providers you have paid to purchase their curriculum. And copy from books of high school course descriptions. If you own my book, *Setting the Records Straight*, you have my permission to use the course descriptions in it. You can also use your own curriculum suppliers' course descriptions.

3. Avoid plagiarism by using the Starbucks Method.

You can avoid plagiarism when writing course descriptions by first learning and understanding the course description, then rewriting it in your own words. I call this "The Starbucks Method." Read the descriptions. Sip your latte. Nibble your cookie. Spin around three times in your chair. Then write the description in your own words, so it sounds like you.

Remember, you don't have to worry about plagiarism if you purchase my book, *Setting the Records Straight*, or my Comprehensive Record Solution, because you have my permission to use the course descriptions in these resources, as written. You only need to modify them to fit your own grades.

4. Describe delight directed learning.

Include course descriptions for delight directed learning. Course descriptions are important for every class—they are not more important or less important for physical education, occupational education, or math. Particularly when you are compensating for average test scores, you want to show the rigor of your homeschool classes through these course descriptions. They can include the various hands-on activities for each class, such as field trips, workshops, and jobs. Convert natural learning into high school credit with my free eBook at homescholar.homehighschoolhelp.com/delight-directed-learning-white-paper.

5. Imitate a school syllabus.

There is nothing new under the sun and no matter how unusual your class may be, chances are there is a high school somewhere in the United States offering a similar class. Fortunately, you have a special, scientific magical look up machine called Google. When you are truly stumped, search for the keyword, such as "ranching" and add the words "high school course description" or "high school syllabus" to find a similar class. Then imitate their words and review their grading criteria for ideas (if you didn't grade the class as your child was engaging in the delight directed learning).

6. Cover letters explain unusual situations.

Use a cover letter to introduce or explain tough situations you don't want to include on the transcript or in the course descriptions. My cover letter was a simple introduction, "Enclosed are the comprehensive homeschool records for my son, Kevin Binz." But a cover letter can be your best friend if you need to explain complicated situations, such as taking five years to finish high school, health troubles, failing grades, or changes in school situations.

Perfect Record Keeping Not Required

Perfect record keeping means keeping records, including creating course descriptions. It does not mean you have perfectly kept, tidy records. You don't have to be perfect, grade everything, or even continue the same curriculum for a full year. Beautiful notebooks aren't required either, if simple lined paper or leftover graph paper will suffice. You don't need to always use the same colored pen or pencil, or even include test grades in every subject.

If you look closely at my own records, you'll notice I spelled "Reading" incorrectly. My children also did so poorly on reading tests, I stopped giving them. I only graded three subjects one year: math, foreign language, and history. In fact, every year I only graded with tests when the curriculum came with tests. I never used a specific pen or pencil. You can almost see my monthly mood swings on each entry.

But, can we discuss the results for a moment? Even though my records weren't perfect, I used them to create transcripts and course descriptions. My children still graduated. They still got into and succeeded in college! They managed to get marvelous scholarships, too.

Perfect record keeping isn't about keeping records perfectly. The homeschooler with the prettiest records doesn't win. Perfect record keeping is just **doing** it. Simply be sure you are keeping the records. When parents are finished homeschooling their children, what I hear most is not "I wish I wouldn't have done that," or "Wow, that was a huge pain!" What I hear most often is shock and awe! Parents are shocked at the wonderful results and amazed at the family closeness.

Course Descriptions Earn Scholarships

Kristen started out thinking, "Could this seriously become a reality for us?" and ended up with a full tuition scholarship.

"During the first webinar of yours that I ever joined when my daughter was a freshman, I learned that your sons received full tuition scholarships to their top choice university. I asked myself

'Could this seriously become a reality for us?' In the fervent hopes that it could, I devoted months of my time to capturing our daughter's amazing high school education. I closely followed your advice from webinars, the Total Transcript [Solution] and Comprehensive Record Solution, and e-books on how to how to best piece her educational picture together. It paid off! Our daughter just learned that she was awarded a full tuition scholarship to her top choice university, too! A thousand thanks to you and the help that you so graciously provide!"

~ Kristen (Minnesotan mom living overseas)

She was not alone in her success. Sharon wrote to me to share the big scholarships that her daughter received.

"My daughter was offered a total of $232,000 in scholarships at this time. We followed all of your tips about course descriptions. Rachel has done a lot of independent learning and had many different interests. That was reflected in her transcripts. I will say the colleges loved the course descriptions. I had someone tell me the colleges did not want all that information but it made a difference for her."

~ Sharon in Texas

The National Association for College Admission Counseling, NACAC, emphasizes the importance of taking challenging classes. "Year to year, we find that getting good grades in challenging courses is what college admission offices value most when reviewing applications from first-time freshmen," said Joyce E. Smith, NACAC's chief executive officer (hub.nacacnet.org/NC__Login).

"Performance in core classes is especially significant, with 79.2 percent of institutions attributing 'considerable importance' to grades in college-prep courses."

Students should take a balanced load— one that allows them to devote the necessary time to each class, because colleges look for quality, not quantity. According to Dan Saracino, former assistant provost for enrollment at the University of Notre Dame, "Nothing is more important than the quality of the course load."

So, how do you convince colleges of the academic rigor of each class? And how do you show your child's performance in your rigorous class?

Course descriptions are the answer. I hope this helps you think through course descriptions and why they're important to your child's college admissions packet.

Unfortunately, you need to do the work of writing course descriptions to help your child earn scholarships. I would love to help you with this task. You know how homeschool parents think about their children's learning styles? Well, I think about your learning style! So, if you would like more help with course descriptions, take my free class on **Homeschool Records that Open Doors** on my website under "Freebies".

If you are super stressed or need a quick read, purchase my easy-reading book on Amazon that describes how to create records, *Comprehensive Homeschool Records: Put Your Best Foot Forward to Win College Admission and Scholarships.* When you are ready to create course descriptions, you may want to purchase the Comprehensive Record Solution. It includes everything you need from multiple training classes, to templates and descriptions you can cut and paste into your own course descriptions.

Afterword

Who is Lee Binz and What Can She Do for Me?

Number one best-selling homeschool author, Lee Binz is The HomeScholar. Her mission is "helping parents homeschool high school." Lee and her husband, Matt, homeschooled their two boys, Kevin and Alex, from elementary through high school.

Upon graduation, both boys received four-year, full tuition scholarships from their first choice university. This enables Lee to pursue her dream job—helping parents homeschool their children through high school.

On The HomeScholar website, you will find great products for creating homeschool transcripts and comprehensive records to help you amaze and impress colleges.

Find out why Andrew Pudewa, Founder of the Institute for Excellence in Writing says, "Lee Binz knows how to navigate this often confusing and frustrating labyrinth better than anyone."

You can find Lee online at:

HomeHighSchoolHelp.com

If this book has been helpful, could you please take a minute to write us a quick review on Amazon? Thank you!

Testimonials

I felt totally equipped

The Home Scholar is excellent! Before I visited her website, I was nervous about making transcripts and documenting high school courses. After I listened to her free webinars and read her free articles, I felt totally equipped to make a transcript and other necessary documents needed for the college admission process. She also made it easy to determine what courses our kids needed to take for a college prep education. Her free resources were so helpful that I was eager to purchase the Total Transcript Solution and the Comprehensive

Record Solution products, and I have been very pleased with those as well.

~ Jenn

She shared great ideas

Lee Binz at the HomeScholar is fabulous! Without making me feel inferior, Lee helped me complete my son's transcript. While in her Gold Club, she shared **great** ideas about how to get around details that were really worrying me.

I only used the Gold Club for two months and stopped membership because that's all I needed. When I left (until the future when my next child will be graduating), nobody at The HomeScholar gave me any grief or guilt trips because I was leaving. It was more like "see you later!"

Thanks Lee for sharing your homeschooling to college gifts with others!

~ Ana

For more information about my **Total Transcript Solution** and **Gold Care Club**, go to:

www.TotalTranscriptSolution.com
www.GoldCareClub.com

Also From The HomeScholar...

- The HomeScholar Guide to College Admission and Scholarships: Homeschool Secrets to Getting Ready, Getting In and Getting Paid (Book and Kindle Book)

- Setting the Records Straight—How to Craft Homeschool Transcripts and Course Descriptions for College Admission and Scholarships (Book and Kindle Book)

- TechnoLogic: How to Set Logical Technology Boundaries and Stop the Zombie Apocalypse

- Finding the Faith to Homeschool High School: Weekly Reflections for Weary Parents

- The HomeScholar Bookshelf (Collection of Print Books)

- Total Transcript Solution (Online Training, Tools and Templates)

- Comprehensive Record Solution (Online Training, Tools and Templates)

- High School Solution (Comprehensive Training, Tools, Resources, and Support)

- College Launch Solution (Comprehensive Training, Tools, Resources, and Support)

- Gold Care Club (Comprehensive Online Support and Training)

- Silver Training Club (Online Training)

- Parent Training Classes (Online Training)

The HomeScholar Coffee Break Books Released or Coming Soon on Kindle and Paperback:

- Delight Directed Learning: Guiding Your Homeschooler Toward Passionate Learning

- Creating Transcripts for Your Unique Child: Help Your Homeschool Graduate Stand Out from the Crowd

- Beyond Academics: Preparation for College and for Life

- Planning High School Courses: Charting the Course Toward High School Graduation

- Graduate Your Homeschooler in Style: Make Your Homeschool Graduation Memorable

- Keys to High School Success: Get Your Homeschool High School Started Right!

- Getting the Most Out of Your Homeschool This Summer: Learning just for the Fun of it!

- Finding a College: A Homeschooler's Guide to Finding a Perfect Fit

- College Scholarships for High School Credit: Learn and Earn With This Two-for-One Strategy!

- College Admission Policies Demystified: Understanding Homeschool Requirements for Getting In

- A Higher Calling: Homeschooling High School for Harried Husbands (by Matt Binz, Mr. HomeScholar)

- Gifted Education Strategies for Every Child: Homeschool Secrets for Success

- College Application Essays: A Primer for Parents

- Creating Homeschool Balance: Find Harmony Between Type A and Type Zzz...

- Homeschooling the Holidays: Sanity Saving Strategies and Gift Giving Ideas

- Your Goals this Year: A Year by Year Guide to Homeschooling High School

- Making the Grades: A Grouch-Free Guide to Homeschool Grading

- High School Testing: Knowledge That Saves Money

- Getting the BIG Scholarships: Learn Expert Secrets for Winning College Cash!

- Easy English for Simple Homeschooling: How to Teach, Assess and Document High School English

- Scheduling—The Secret to Homeschool Sanity: Plan You Way Back to Mental Health

- Junior Year is the Key to High School Success: How to Unlock the Gate to Graduation and Beyond

- Upper Echelon Education: How to Gain Admission to Elite Universities

- How to Homeschool College: Save Time, Reduce Stress and Eliminate Debt

- Homeschool Curriculum That's Effective and Fun: Avoid the Crummy Curriculum Hall of Shame!

- Comprehensive Homeschool Records: Put Your Best Foot Forward to Win College Admission and Scholarships

- Options After High School: Steps to Success for College or Career

- How to Homeschool 9th and 10th Grades: Simple Steps for Starting Strong!

- Senior Year Step-by-Step: Simple Instructions for Busy Homeschool Parents

- How to Homeschool Independently: Do-it-Yourself Secrets to Rekindle the Love of Learning

- High School Math The Easy Way: Simple Strategies for Homeschool Parents in Over Their Heads

- Homeschooling Middle School with Powerful Purpose: How to Successfully Navigate 6th through 8th Grades

- Simple Science for Homeschooling High School: Because Teaching Science isn't Rocket Science!

- How to Be Your Child's Best College Coach: Strategies for Success Using Teens You'll Find Lying Around the House

Would you like to be notified when we offer the next *Coffee Break Books* for FREE during our Kindle promotion days? If so, leave your name and email below and we will send you a reminder.

HomeHighSchoolHelp.com/
freekindlebook

Visit my Amazon Author Page!
amazon.com/author/leebinz

Made in the USA
Las Vegas, NV
14 December 2023

82346272R00075